Parents That Pray

From a Teacher's Perspective

CALLIE ECHOLS STALLIARD

WESTBOW
PRESS®
A DIVISION OF THOMAS NELSON
& ZONDERVAN

WestBow Press books may be ordered through booksellers or by contacting:

WestBow Press
A Division of Thomas Nelson & Zondervan
1663 Liberty Drive
Bloomington, IN 47403
www.westbowpress.com
844-714-3454

ISBN: 978-1-6642-9270-3 (sc)
ISBN: 978-1-6642-9327-4 (hc)
ISBN: 978-1-6642-9271-0 (e)

Library of Congress Control Number: 2023903122

Print information available on the last page.

WestBow Press rev. date: 03/02/2023

Contents

Introduction

Many people ask, what can be done to help improve our schools? More than anything, schools, teachers, classrooms, and even society as a whole need parents that pray. I mean, really praying, seeking God on a regular basis. The problems are huge and there are many of them. So many problems that we don't know where to start or what to do. So, we must pray. He will show us what to do! Many times, we want to leave God out. We cannot do this without God.

We must utilize one of the greatest privileges as believers and communicate regularly with God. How do we communicate with God? The answer is through prayer.

We cannot begin to imagine what our schools would be like if all parents that know Jesus Christ would begin to make it one of their main missions in life to get a serious prayer life. Our children are exposed to some very dangerous times. Some of the most dangerous times in history. Times when school shootings and bullying is tragically almost commonplace. We need to be seriously praying over our children like never before; and seeking God like we've never done.

I know that a lot of people do pray for and over their children. So, I'm not saying any of this from a high and mighty position. I too need prayer. That's one of the reasons why I pray so much. In spending time with God, it becomes ever more evident that I am nothing without Him. That if it had not been for His grace and mercy, I don't know where I would be. I know without a shadow of a doubt, that people prayed for me. I also know that He answers prayer.

Jesus Christ and the Holy Spirit are the Master Teachers. Jesus showed us by example how to do this thing called life and the Holy Spirit works with us (body, mind, and spirit) each day. He never leaves. He knows us and He is the Great Counselor. Any teacher knows you are more than just a teacher; you're often times a counselor. Teachers know how very important it is to not just tell, but to show as well. Jesus simplified many things for people to where they could understand. Often, they are called parables. He not only told, but He showed and demonstrated, and through the Holy Spirit, He is able to help and counsel us.

Through prayer and staying close to Him and working with Him, He can help us with everything we need. There's nothing He can't do and there's nothing He can't change.

He is to be exalted, honored, and revered above everything else. Parents that pray must recognize or remember and become ever more cognizant of the magnitude of God and the power of prayer.

Privilege of Prayer

Lesson Topic: Privilege

Vocabulary: privilege, righteous

Scripture(s):   Matthew 7:7; Philippians 4:6; Mark 11:24; James 5:16

Lesson: Prayer is a gift from God our Father. It is a great expression of love that the Creator has given us as a way to communicate with Him. It is incredible that God would want to talk with us. He can read our minds and our hearts. He knows what we stand in the need of before we even ask. But I've come to realize that it is an expression of how much He cares and loves us that He wants to hear from us.

God is a gentleman. He wants to help us, but He will not force His way into our lives. Scriptures tell us to ask and it shall be given to us. It instructs us to not be anxious about anything, but in every situation, to present our requests to God. It also says, "Whatever we ask for in prayer, believe that we have received it, and it shall be ours" (Matthew 7:7; Philippians 4:6; Mark 11:24 NIV).

Wow! What a privilege that is! There is great power in prayer. James 5:16 says, "The prayer of a righteous person (a believer) is powerful and effective." What is a privilege? It is a right or benefit that is given to some people. As believers we have been given the right to pray.

Summary: We all could benefit from increasing our prayer time and spending more time with God. There is nothing that we can't talk to Him about. There is nothing that He doesn't already know. There is nothing that He can't help with or fix. All things are possible with God.

The Bible is filled with people who sought God in prayer and who received tremendous results. One of our problems today, especially in Western culture, is that we like results right away. It is difficult to wait for anything. Most times when you pray, you may not see the results right away. That doesn't mean that God isn't working. But we lose patience and faith when God does not answer us as quickly as we would like. But one thing hasn't changed; when we have a tragedy, we will once again revisit our privilege, as children of the Most High God, to pray. We need to practice this privilege much more often.

Encouragement: Parents, you have been given an awesome responsibility. What a privilege to be able to talk with God in prayer about anything and everything. He knows you. He made you. He knows everything. You can trust that what you tell Him, will be kept between you and Him. Your kids lean and depend on you for everything. What a blessing it is that you have a Father in Heaven that you can lean and depend on for everything.

Prayer: Lord God Most High,
Thank You for the privilege of prayer. Thank You that You care enough that You want to hear from us. You desire to help us whenever and wherever we need You. Help us Lord, to ask for what we need, to pray about everything that concerns us, and help us to believe that what we have prayed for, we have received it from You. Help us Lord to better understand that prayer is a privilege from You and that we are to use our privilege more often. Thank You Lord that You are already working in our lives. In Jesus' name we pray. Amen!

Parents That Pray Know God

Lesson Topic: Knowing God

Vocabulary: know

Scripture(s):   Colossians 1:10; Colossians 2:2-3

Lesson: Parents that pray know God. Definitions of "know" include to be acquainted with or to understand from experience or attainment. It is wise to learn and understand more about God. Scripture says, "This will help you live in a way that brings honor to the Lord and pleases Him in every way; that your life will produce good works of every kind and that you will grow in your knowledge of God" Colossians 1:10 (Easy-to-Read Version).

It can sometimes be of help to not only look at scriptures about who God is, but to also look at facts about His creation. That includes not only these amazing human bodies that we operate in but also investigating and doing short research about the world He has created.

I'm no scientist, but after doing a little research I learned a few tid bits worth mentioning about God's creations. The largest bone in the human body is the femur. It can support 30 times the weight of a person's body. Ounce for ounce, that's stronger than steel.[1] Messages from the human brain travel along nerves at up to 200 miles an hour (322 km/h).[1] If a human being's DNA were uncoiled, it would stretch 10 billion miles, from Earth to Pluto and back.[1] The atmosphere around us is made up of two main ingredients— nitrogen and oxygen—whose mixture is always the same, whether at the highest mountaintops or in the deepest caves. The perfect balance is 79 percent nitrogen and 21 percent oxygen. It is important that we have this exact mixture of nitrogen and oxygen. God made it just right. This world would become chaotic if this atmospheric

---

[1] https://www.factretriever.com/body-facts

mixture slipped out of control for just a single instant. We would see one of the most tremendous of all explosions, because nitrogen is the basic component of gunpowder; and oxygen, of course, makes for rapid combustion. It would be "Goodbye, world!"[2]

I could go on stating the amazing facts about our human bodies and the universe. It would be worth doing your own research to give you a little better perspective about how amazing our God is. When we spend time learning about God it gives us more insight on how great this God is who we believe in and serve. It increases and deepens our relationship with God. This God that we serve wants to have a relationship with us. He wants us to know Him more. Jesus died so that our relationship could be restored with the Father. He wants to be a part of our life and live life with us. We must re-energize our relationships with God so

---

[2] https://www.amazingfacts.org/media-library/book/e/1/t/amazing-wonders-of-creation

that He can do the work in us that needs to be done. So that we can live the best lives that He has prepared for us. Having good relationships are not easy. They take time. Parents that pray have to carve out time to get to know God so that their relationship can grow.

There are benefits in knowing God. Colossians 2:2-3 from the Amplified Bible says, "[For my hope is] that their hearts may be encouraged as they are knit together in [unselfish] love, so that they may have all the riches that come from the full assurance of understanding [the joy of salvation], resulting in a true [and more intimate] knowledge of the mystery of God, *that is*, Christ in whom are hidden all the treasures of wisdom and knowledge [regarding the word and purposes of God]."

Summary: There are many benefits listed in those two scriptures. The first being that our hearts will be encouraged. If ever there was a time that hearts needed to be encouraged, this is the time. When we spend time with God, getting to know Him, our hearts will be refreshed. Next, we will be knit together in unselfish love. Wow. The world is in desperate need of unselfish love. The third benefit in those scriptures can be complex, but respectively and simply saying, that we can find wisdom and knowledge for the purposes of God for our lives through having a more intimate knowledge of Him and Christ Jesus.

From a teacher's perspective, children need parents that pray and know The Lord. Schools need parents that know God. Schools need parents that spend time with God. Our schools need more parents that are encouraged, love unselfishly, and know Jesus Christ. Schools need parents that pray!

Encouragement: Parents you are an amazing creation created by an amazing God.

Prayer: Thank You God for who You are. Thank You that You are a God who wants us to know and understand You more. Help us to learn more about You in practical ways that we can comprehend. Give us ideas of ways to learn more about You so that we can live lives that are more pleasing to You. Thank You that You are enabling us to learn more about You so that we can live lives that produce good works that bring honor to You. We thank You in advance for working in our lives. In Jesus' name we pray. Amen!

Parents That Pray Study The Word

Lesson Topic: Studying The Word of GOD

Vocabulary: study, lamp, light, path

Scripture(s):   Psalm 119:105

Lesson: Some of the verb definitions of study is to apply oneself, to think deeply, or to take a course in something. Studying The Word of God is important because when you apply yourself to something or think deeply about a topic, or dive into a topic deeper; as to taking a course in it; it becomes better understood. You get new knowledge as to the inner workings or a deeper understanding of its importance.

The same is true when we study The Word of God. God's Word is a living and applicable resource for our lives. You would not expect your children to do well for a test if they have not studied. The same is true for the tests in our own lives. Scripture says, "Your Word is a lamp for my feet and a light on my path." The dictionary says that a lamp is a source of intellectual or spiritual light. A light is something that makes things visible.

So, the Word of God is like a source of intellectual or spiritual light to my feet and something that makes things visible to my path.

Studying the Word of God does not require you to leave your home or spend lots of money. All you need is a prayer asking God for His blessing on your time spent and for Him to cause you to see what He wants you to see and know what He wants you to know. Grab your Bible, dictionary/thesaurus, and a notepad. Look up one scripture and write down all the significant words in that scripture. Even if it's every word. Before you know it, you will have a deeper understanding of what you have read.

Summary: I must confess. I have not always studied the Word of God like I should. But without a doubt, when I carve out the time (even 20 minutes) to study a scripture, how much more His Word means to me. The great thing is God does not have a requirement on how much time we need to spend studying His Word. He just helps me get a better understanding of His Word and somehow it results in my spirit being encouraged.

Parents need not only this spiritual light for themselves to handle all that a parent must handle, but also for your kids. Kids need not just their parents to be a spiritual light, but they also need prayer over their lives that they will receive the light and lamp they need for their own pathways in life.

Encouragement: Parents, you are gifted providers for your children, a light for them. It is vital that you receive light from the Father through His Word.

Prayer: Lord God,
                   Thank You for all that You are in our lives.
                   Thank You that You are the light, and
                   You know the path that we need to take.
                   Help us to study Your Word with a deeper
                   understanding. Make our understanding
                   clear and give us holy insight of what you
                   want us to do. Give us simple steps of how
                   we can begin to study and understand Your
                   Word more. We thank You in advance for
                   Your plan for our lives. We thank You in
                   advance for all the knowledge that You
                   are enabling us to receive. Thank You
                   that You said through Your Word we will
                   receive light for our paths. In Jesus' name
                   we pray. Amen!

Parents That Pray
Believe God's Word

Lesson Topic: Believing God's Word

Vocabulary: believe, faith

Scripture(s):   Hebrews 11:6; Proverbs 3:5-6

Lesson: The dictionary states that the word believe means "to have confidence in the truth, the existence, or the re-liability of something." Some people have difficulty having confidence in God's Word and Promises, because they simply are not sure of His Word or His Promises. One benefit from studying The Word of God is that you have an understanding of what His Word says. It's hard to have confidence in something or someone that you are not sure what they are all about.

Hebrews 11:6 says, "Without faith it is impossible to please God, because anyone who comes to Him must believe that He exists and that He rewards those who earnestly seek Him." Faith is confidence or trust in God to do what He has promised.

It is often tough trusting God because He rarely does things how or when we think He needs to. But Scripture also reminds us to "Trust in the Lord with all your heart and lean not on your own understanding; in all your ways submit to Him, and He will make your paths straight" (Proverbs 3:5-6).

Summary:

Kids need parents that are not only praying, but also believing the Word of God. A parent that is praying and believing God is a mighty warrior in the life of their children. Kids walk out of their homes every day into a world that is in chaos. They are faced with dangers seen and unseen, as my grandmother used to say. Children need parents who are praying and believing God to protect them and keep them safe. Children need parents who are praying and believing God to help them make good decisions. A warrior is someone who is engaged or experienced in warfare. Children need parents who are engaged in spiritual warfare through prayer to protect them from the evil one. "The one who," scripture says, "comes only to steal, kill, and destroy" (John 10:10). These prayers combined with the belief of children's parents are priceless to students.

Encouragement: Parents your belief in God's Word changes things. It changes lives, circumstances, and outcomes. Your belief is vitally important to your child's success.

Prayer: Lord,
                 Thank You that You are a God Who not only makes promises but keeps Your Promises. You are faithful to Your Word and to us. Help us, God, to not only pray but believe Your Promises. Help us to study Your Promises and to meditate on them with great expectation. Help us

not to lean on our own understanding, but to believe that You know all about our situation and that You are working even while we don't see the changes just yet. Help us to be pleasing to You as we wait for You to come through for us. We believe that You do exist and that You are a rewarder of those who diligently seek You. We thank You that You are a rewarder! Your Word says in Psalm 86:10, "For You are great and do marvelous deeds; You alone are God." We believe in You! In Jesus' name we pray. Amen!

Parents That Pray Speak the Word of God

Lesson Topic: Speaking the Word of God

Vocabulary: speak, power

Scripture(s):   John 8:28; Proverbs 18:21; Isaiah 55:11

Lesson: One of Jesus' assignments on earth was to show us how to live. In John 8:28 Jesus says, "When You have lifted up the Son of Man, then you will know that I am He, and that I do nothing on My own, but speak just what the Father has taught Me." Jesus always exalted The Father, and, in this verse, we examine that He spoke the things that God taught Him. It is very important for us to watch what we say. More importantly, to watch what we say about ourselves, our circumstances, and our loved ones.

Proverbs 18:21 says, "The tongue has the power of life and death." What does that really mean? A definition of power is the ability to do or act or the capability of doing or accomplishing something. Simply put, what we say about our situations, or our children has the ability to become or accomplish exactly what we have spoken.

It is vital for kids to hear positivity spoken about them and their situations continuously. I'm not talking about exaggerating or blowing their egos up. I'm talking about stating the truth about a situation but declaring God's Word about it in the end. For example: If a child struggles in math, instead of just saying to them, "I know you've always struggled with math, and I guess that's the way it is." You can say, "I know you've always struggled in math, but God has promised that He will supply our every need. So that includes you being able to do well in math. We are going to believe God for that and ask Him to lead us in getting you the help you need to do better in math."

Summary: We must be careful about what we speak about our situations. One definition for the word speak is to express and make known. We all need to think about what we are expressing and making known. Are we expressing and making known the Word and Promises of God or are we expressing and making known our emotions and feelings at the time?

It is a very powerful thing for a child to have the Word of God spoken over their lives continually. We may not see the work being done in them at the time, but God's Word is true, and the Bible says, "it will not return to Him empty" (Isaiah 55:11).

Encouragement: Parents you are ambassadors for your children and their futures. You have the power to declare and announce to the future, this wonderful, talented person to come. Use your belief in God and His Promises to speak words of blessings over your children.

Prayer: Lord God,

Thank You that Your Word is true and that You do not lie. Thank You for teaching us that our words are important and powerful. Thank You that when we go through difficult times, instead of restating our situation, we can speak Your Word over it; knowing that there is power in Your Word to change our circumstances. Help us Lord, when we don't see immediate change that we will continue speaking Your Word over our issues believing that You are already at work. Thank You that there is nothing too hard for You and that there is nothing You can't change. We thank You in advance for the answers to our problems and concerns. In Jesus' name we pray. Amen!

Parents That Pray – Pray Scriptures

Lesson Topic: Praying Scriptures

Vocabulary: pray; ask

Scripture(s):   Matthew 7:11

Lesson: One of the best attributes of parents is that they want to give their children good gifts. Matthew 7:11 says, "That if you then know how to give good gifts to your children, how much more will your Father in Heaven give good gifts to those who ask Him."

It can be helpful to make a list of some concerns for our children, make a list of the scriptures that deal with those concerns, and pray those scriptures. Another word for prayer is petition. A petition means a formally drawn request, or a request made for something desired.

I discovered a website of 12 powerful scriptures to pray over our children by Lisa Jacobsen. In this article, the top 3 concerns are: strength, courage, and peace. Children need strength to live in this world. We can pray Philippians 4:13 over them which says, "they can do all things through Him Who gives them strength." Children need courage to act as they have been taught and to handle all they will face. Joshua 1:9 reminds them "to be strong and courageous and to not be afraid because the Lord their God will be with them wherever they go." Philippians 4:6 gives them instructions on how to have peace.

Summary: Praying scriptures gives parents an assurance that their prayers are being heard. The prayer or petition is specific, and it is a promise from God. When we pray scriptures, it is putting God in remembrance of His Word. I once heard it described like this, "God, You said in Philippians 4:13 that they can do all things through Christ Jesus Who strengthens them. You said, O Lord in Joshua 1:9 that they are to be strong and courageous and to not be afraid for You will be with them wherever they go. So, Lord I am depending on You. You said for them not to be anxious about anything, but in every situation, by prayer and petition, with thanksgiving, present our request to You. And the peace of God which transcends all understanding, will guard our hearts and our minds, according to Philippians 4:6."

Encouragement: Parents praying scriptures are extremely powerful. Students need encouragement all throughout the day. Many kids have been taught the right things to do, but they need strength, courage, and peace to act those things out. Those prayers allow God to work mightily in their lives.

Prayer: Dear Lord,
Thank You for not only the privilege of prayer, but also teaching us how to pray. Thank You Lord that when we pray Your Word, it not only changes things, but it also

changes us. It empowers us, it encourages us, and strengthens us to continue to believe and wait on You, knowing that You are true to Your Word and Your Promises. Thank You Lord that we can be strong and courageous no matter what we face because You said in Deuteronomy 31:6, "So be strong and courageous! Do not be afraid or terrified because of them. For the Lord Your God goes with you. He will neither leave you nor forsake you." You said in Isaiah 54:17 that "no weapon formed against us will prevail." You said, "You would withhold no good thing from those who walk uprightly or do what is right" (Psalm 84:11-NLT). You said in 1 Chronicles 16:12 (KJV), that "You do marvelous things for Your people." So, we stand on Your Word Lord. We believe Your Word Lord. Thank You for working in our lives. In Jesus' Name. Amen!

Parents That Pray Seek God's Direction

Lesson Topic: Seeking God's Direction

Vocabulary: wisdom

Scripture(s):   James 1:5

Lesson: Have you ever felt like you didn't know what to do? Have you ever felt like you didn't know how to help your child do something? Often times in life we are faced with situations that we simply don't know what to do. James 1:5 (AMP) tells us that, "If any of you lacks wisdom [to guide him through a decision or circumstance], he is to ask of [our benevolent] God, who gives to everyone generously and without rebuke *or* blame, and it will be given to him".

We are given a promise from God that He will give us wisdom because we have asked. Sometimes our first instinct is to try to figure out things without consulting and without seeking wisdom from God. We think we know what to do based on past experiences, but those experiences are exactly that, from the past. What we used in a prior situation may not be what is needed in future situations. God may have other avenues for us take or use. We must be careful to humble ourselves and ask for God's direction in every situation.

Summary: Parents may not always know exactly what to do with a difficult child or a struggling student, but with prayer, God promises to give wisdom to those that ask. God has many ways to give us understanding and wisdom. It doesn't always come in the form you may expect, so we have to keep our eyes and ears open expecting God to give us the answer at any time.

Not only do we expect Him to answer, but we must also be willing to act when He tells us what to do.

Encouragement: Parents, what a blessing it is to seek the Lord in prayer and to ask for wisdom for any and every situation. You don't have to pretend with God. You don't have to feel bad or discouraged because you don't have the answer. Turn to the Lord. Be honest with Him and ask for wisdom in handling your issue. Ask for guidance and for obedience and clarity in carrying out His instructions.

Prayer: Father God,
We thank You for the promise that if we don't know what to do, You will give us wisdom. Thank You that You don't look down on us for asking and that You don't even expect us to know it all. Thank You that You want us to come to You for help. You said, You were our ever-present help in our time of need. Thank You Lord, that we can depend on You for holy wisdom and guidance. Lord, help us to

act on what You tell us to do. Help us to humble ourselves to be open to Your guidance and directions. Thank You Lord in advance for leading and guiding us. In Jesus' Name we pray. Amen!

Parents That Pray Ask For God's Grace

Lesson Topic: Asking For God's Grace

Vocabulary: grace

Scripture(s):   2 Corinthians 12:9; Hebrews 4:16

Lesson: Raising children can be a taxing assignment. Many parents find it difficult to provide all a child needs and have peace. The never-ending list of trying to provide for their physical needs, their emotional needs, working a full-time job, and taking care of the house can be quite daunting at times. Many parents feel overwhelmed and oftentimes too aware of their weaknesses.

2 Corinthians 12:9 tells us that "His grace is sufficient for us; for His power is made perfect in weakness." One of the

definitions for grace is favor or goodwill. Parents need to sometimes ask for God's grace in helping them deal with raising children. The pressure is great in trying to be a good parent. Grace is His help and His favor in assisting us.

Summary: Our weaknesses show us two things. They show us just how much we need God, and the other thing is how great God's power is. God promises us that His grace is sufficient or enough. When we depend on His grace, He will give us what we need to handle what we need to handle. When He brings us through a situation, we can look back at it in awe knowing that it was God's power at work not our own strength.

Hebrews 4:16 encourages us "To approach God's throne of grace with confidence, so that we may receive mercy and find grace to help us in our time of need." We have the privilege of going to God with confidence knowing that there is nothing He can't help us with. We must know that there is nothing too big for Him.

Encouragement: It is okay and natural to feel weak and unqualified at times. The good news is that our Father's grace is more powerful than our weaknesses. He promises that His grace and His assistance will be all that need. We must go to Him in prayer and acknowledge our weaknesses and then boldly let Him know that we are depending on His strength to get us through.

Prayer: Lord,

How we thank You for Your awesome grace and power. Your Word says that Your grace is sufficient for us; that Your power is made perfect in our weakness. Thank You that You know about our weaknesses and that You provide grace and power. What a Mighty God You are that You know about our weaknesses before we do and that You have already provided. How wonderful it is to know that even in our very weakness that Your power works on our behalf. Your Word says in Romans 8:28 that "in all things God works for the good of those who love

Him, who have been called according to His purpose." All things include our weaknesses, and we are so grateful. Give us the grace to have peace and joy in raising our children. We approach Your Throne of Grace in confidence because You instruct us to; so, we expect good things. Not because we deserve them, but because You are good and do marvelous things for Your people. We love You Lord. In Jesus' name we pray. Amen!

Parents That Pray Know That Group Prayer Is Important

Lesson Topic: The Importance of Group/Corporate Prayer

Vocabulary: agree, corporate

Scripture(s): Matthew 18:19-20

Lesson: Parents that pray are vitally important. Parents that are praying together with other believers are unstoppable. Jesus tells us that "If two of us here on earth agree about anything they ask for, it will be done by the Father in Heaven." He also says, "Where two or three gather in My name, there am I with them" (Matthew 18:19-20).

To agree means to have similar views about something. If we agree that we have faith in God, if we agree that there is nothing too big for God, if we agree that we have a need from God, it would be in our best interest to pray and believe together. There is great power in praying together. Another word for praying together is corporate prayer. The dictionary says a meaning for corporate is united. When we are united in prayer, the bible promises that what we are asking for will be done for us and that He would be there in our midst.

Summary:

Why don't we do this more often? Are we too busy? We cannot afford to be too busy. A benefit in praying together is added strength and encouragement. You may be feeling worn out and another believer can pray, and you are able to receive strength and encouragement, maybe rejuvenation from the prayers of the group members.

Children need parents who will come together regularly to pray over them, their futures, their decisions, and their choices. They need the power available through corporate prayer.

Encouragement: How exciting and encouraging it is to know that our Father values and honors group prayer. How wonderful it is to know that "when we pray with others in the name of Jesus," He said, "He would be there with us" (Matthew 18:20). How comforting it is to know and believe that He said, "If two of us agree about anything that it will be done for us by our Father in Heaven" (Matthew 18:19).

Prayer: Dear Lord,

Thank You for Your Word which promises us that if we agree in prayer with one another that not only will You be in our midst, but that what we ask You for, it will be done for us by The Father in Heaven. Help us Lord, to realize and understand what great power is available in group/corporate prayer. Thank You Lord, for giving us these avenues to aid us in getting our prayers answered. Thank You for continuing to work in each of our lives and in our circumstances. In Jesus' Name we pray. Amen!

Parents That Pray Train Their Children

Lesson Topic: Training Your Children

Vocabulary: train

Scripture(s):   Proverbs 22:6

Lesson: Training a child how to do something is quite the task. Training a child how to act and behave is probably one of the most critical points and issues in our schools. In today's society, hearing a child use good manners causes that child to stand out. Something as simple as saying please and thank you are trainable points that are far too often overlooked.

For the child who uses good manners, it causes others to take notice. It not only puts the child in a favorable light, but it also makes others think that their parents have surely been training them. In order to train, repetition is involved to develop a habit. It is the constant reinforcement of how to do something. Everything we expect our students to do has to be taught. Then it must be reinforced. Often times it has to also be explained. More often this training takes a lot of time and patience.

Summary:

Proverbs 22:6 tells parents "To start children off in the way they should go, and when they are old, they will not turn from it." Parents that pray are probably already doing this. It must not go unmentioned that the training you are doing is not in vain. Training can often take much longer than we might expect.

Children are oftentimes products of their training. If a child does something well, most of the time, they have been trained well. If they are not doing something well, usually they need more training. Most children have the desire to please. It makes them feel good. If they are consistently not complying that may mean, there needs to be a change in the training. Attributes like knowing how to talk to people, how to treat people, how to clean up after themselves, how to be quiet, how to follow directions, how to read, and how to work hard are too important not to be mastered. If you've not seen the results you would like to see in your training, you need to pray and ask for wisdom on how to go about training your child in that specific area.

From a teacher's perspective, there are rules in this world that must be followed. We are not setting our kids up for success if we don't adequately train them how to behave and why. There are some serious consequences in failing to train up our kids in the way they should go.

Encouragement: The process of training is not an easy task. Whether you are training yourself to eat better, to workout, or to be wiser in your spending, it is not easy and does not come as an overnight success. The good news is that it is possible and with diligence it is attainable. Training takes time, patience, and perseverance. Training children has to be one of the hardest tasks. However, our God does not leave us without help and support. He promises good results for our hard work in training our kids.

Prayer:

Father God,

Thank You for children. Thank You for the joy they can bring and thank You for Your help when they are frustrating to deal with. Thank You that You know what it takes to raise children and that You provide patience, guidance, love, kindness, forgiveness, and faith in order for us to rear them the way that You desire. Give us, Lord, fresh ideas when what we have tried isn't working. Help us to be ever cognizant that our training is not in vain. Make us ever more aware of weaknesses that we need to work on within our children so that they can grow up to be pleasing to You. Give extra strength when we need it. Help us as we continue to lean on You. We trust You Lord because You said, "If we train them how to live, they will remember it all of their lives" (Proverbs 22:6 Easy to Read Version). Thank You for that promise. In Jesus' Name we pray. Amen!

Parents That Pray - Pray Over Their Children

Lesson Topic: Praying Over Your Children

Vocabulary: be, void, fruit

Scripture(s):   Isaiah 55:11; 1 John 5:14: Ephesians 1:17-18

Lesson: God gives parents not only an incredible miracle through children, but also an amazing responsibility. With this responsibility He also gives His Word to be used as a weapon to assist parents in raising children.

The King James Version of Isaiah 55:11 says, "So shall My Word be that goeth forth out of my mouth: it shall not return unto Me void, but it shall accomplish that which I please, and it shall prosper in the thing whereto I sent it."

God says, "So shall His Word be that goes forth out of His mouth." To be, according to the dictionary, means to take place or to happen. He is saying that His Word or promises will take place or will happen and that they will not return unto Him void. The dictionary describes void as useless.

The New Living Translation references Isaiah 5:11 to say, "It is the same with our words. We send it out, and it always produces fruit." The dictionary refers to one definition of fruit as anything produced. What type of fruit do you want to see produced in your child's life? Whatever it is, praying parents pray for those things specifically and regularly.

Summary: From a Praying Teacher's Perspective, students need much prayer to handle all that comes at them on a day-to-day basis. With all that goes on in the daily life of a student, while the hardworking parents are at work, students are in desperate need of prayers that the bible says will produce fruit.

Suggestions for things parents could pray over their children:

- That God will give them the strength to do what they need to do each day because Philippians 4:13 says "they can do all this through Him Who gives them strength."
- That God will provide them with all they need each day because Philippians 4:19 says "My God will meet all your needs according to the riches of His glory in Christ Jesus."
- To be courageous because Joshua 1:9 says "Have I not commanded you? Be strong and courageous. Do not be afraid; do not be discouraged, for the Lord your God will be with you wherever you go."
- To be grateful and thankful because 1 Thessalonians 5:18 says to "Give thanks in all circumstances; for this is God's will for you in Christ Jesus."

- To be joyful because Psalm 16:11 says "God will fill us with joy in His presence."
- To be hopeful for Romans 15:13 says "May the God of hope fill us will all joy and peace as we trust in Him, so that we may overflow with hope by the power of the Holy Spirit."
- To be emotionally stable because 2 Timothy 1:7 (ESV) says "For God gave us a spirit not of fear but of power and love and self-control."
- To have peace for Isaiah 26:3 (ASV) says "He will keep him in perfect peace whose mind is stayed on Him."
- To have compassion for others because Ephesians 4:32 says "Be kind and compassionate to one another, forgiving each other, just as in Christ God forgave you."
- To be courteous; to have and use good manners because Philippians 4:5 says, "Let your gentleness be evident to all. The Lord is near."
- To have a good and positive attitude because Psalm 118:24 says, "The Lord

has done it this very day; let us rejoice today and be glad."

○ To learn/pick-up/comprehend things easily/quickly for Psalm 84:11 says, "For the Lord God is a sun and shield; the Lord bestows favor and honor; no good thing does he withhold from those whose walk is blameless."

○ To be good listeners for James 1:19 says "Everyone should be quick to listen, slow to speak and slow to become angry."

○ To stand-up for what is right and speak out at the appropriate time because Isaiah 1:17 says "Learn to do right; seek justice. Defend the oppressed. Take up the cause of the fatherless; plead the case of the widow."

○ To be quiet when they need to be quiet because Exodus 14:14 says "The Lord will fight for you; you need only to be still."

○ To represent You and GOD well because 2 Corinthians 5:20 says "We are therefore Christ's ambassadors, as though God were making His appeal through us."

o To protect them from evil (comments/ or negative words said against them) because 2 Thessalonians 3:3 says, "But the Lord is faithful, and He will strengthen you and protect you from the evil one."

o To keep them safe for Psalm 16:1 says, "Keep me safe, my God, for in You, I take refuge."

o To help them to make good decisions because Proverbs 2:6 says, "For the Lord gives wisdom; from His mouth come knowledge and understanding."

o Help them to be at the right place at the right time for Psalm 90:17 says, "May the favor of the Lord our God rest on us."

o To give them favor with everyone they come in contact with because Psalm 23:6 says, "Surely your goodness and love will follow me all the days of my life, and I will dwell in the house of the Lord forever."

- To give them good breaks because Psalm 31:19 says, "How abundant are the good things that You have stored up for those who fear You."
- Thank God for the people He is putting in their paths and bless them that they will be good to your child. Psalm 5:12 says "Surely, Lord, You bless the righteous; You surround them with Your favor as with a shield."
- That they will be filled with His love, joy, peace, and hope; and that love, joy, peace, and hope will overflow onto others that others may want to know Christ Jesus because Romans 15:13 says "May the God of hope fill you will all joy and peace as you trust in Him, so that you may overflow with hope by the power of the Holy Spirit."

Encouragement: Parents, God has given you the incredible responsibility of being a holy cheerleader for your children. We know cheerleaders to be sideline encouragers; those who give positive affirmations as the game is being played. As children of God, you not only give words and cheers of encouragement, but your prayers cover your children and cause good fruit to be produced in their lives.

Prayer: Dear Lord,

Thank You for children and thank You for the power of Your Word spoken over them. Thank You for Your Scriptures that when prayed over children can change their lives for the better. We ask that the great God and Father of our Lord Jesus Christ may give them the wisdom of Your Spirit. That they will be able to understand the secrets about You as they know You better. We pray that their hearts will be able to understand. We pray that they will know about the hope given by God's call. We pray that they will see "how great the things are that He has promised to those who belong to Him" (Ephesians 1:17-18 NLV). Thank You Lord that Your Word is not limited; that Your Word covers every situation they may have or being going through. Thank You that all Your promises are for our kids as well. Help us Lord to bring every care that we may have regarding our children to You. Help us to be aware and diligent about praying Your Word over our children regularly. We trust You and believe and stand on Your Word. In Jesus' name we pray. Amen!

Parents That Pray – Pray With Their Children

Lesson Topic: Praying With Children

Vocabulary: habit; listen; near

Scripture(s):   Jeremiah 29:12; Psalm 145:18

Lesson: As I listened to my little niece pray in church one Sunday, I remembered all the mornings riding to school with my mom where she would have us say a prayer. She would start and then like the game Round Robin, we would all take our turn and pray. I can't remember the prayers, but what I realize is the habit it formed in our lives. The dictionary defines the word habit as an acquired behavior pattern regularly followed until it has become almost involuntary.

Jeremiah 29:12 says, "Then you will call on Me and come and pray to Me, and I will listen to you." Our kids need to know that they can call on the Lord and that He will listen. That they have this privilege not only in church but everywhere they go. They need to know that GOD will listen and that He is available even when their parents are not available.

Psalm 145:18 says, "The Lord is near to all who call on Him, to all who call on Him in truth."

Summary: Just like anything else we want our kids to know and do well, they must practice. They must get in the habit of praying. Today, like never before, we need more students in our schools who have the involuntary ability to pray at any time. Parents cannot be with their children all of the time. What a blessing it is to be able to call on the Father for help and to know He is listening and that He is near!

Encouragement: It cannot be stressed enough the importance of building a habit of prayer within your children. One of the most valuable things my parents did for me, was create a foundation of prayer in my life. All of us can look back over our lives at times where there was no one else other than the Lord that we could go to for help.

Parents, you know you cannot go everywhere with your kids, but God does. It is vitally important for your children to have a prayer-life built on the trained habit of communicating with the Father, every day and especially when they are in trouble. Training is not easy. It takes a lot of repetition. But training your children to pray is one of the most valuable things you can do for your kids.

Prayer: Thank You Lord for reminding us to pray with our children. Thank You for making us examples in teaching our children how to pray and the importance of prayer. Thank You that Your eyes are ever watching us and our children and that You are everywhere all of the time, even as we cannot be. Thank You that

You hear the prayers of children and that You want them to pray too. Help us Lord to be good examples as we pray with our children. Help us to develop a habit of praying with our children so that it will become a habit for them. Help us to teach our children that we as parents and guardians cannot be with them physically all the time, but that You, oh Lord are with them always. Thank You that You Lord are omnipresent. That You are everywhere all of the time. Thank You for the comfort that brings us. In Jesus' Name we pray. Amen!

Parents That Pray Are Grateful And Show Gratefulness

Lesson Topic: Being Grateful and Showing Gratefulness

Vocabulary: grateful; show

Scripture(s):   1 Thessalonians 5:18

Lesson: One of the ugliest character traits in a person is ungratefulness. No one likes to see someone who is so concerned about receiving that they do not take the time to be appreciative.

Grateful means to be deeply appreciative of kindness or benefits received. One of parents' biggest aggravations is to have an ungrateful child. However, some of us may find it hard to remember the last time we were deeply appreciative of God's kindness and blessings.

We work really hard and get really busy taking care of the things required in our day-to-day lives. We may say thank you God when we receive, but if we could be very honest, we know that we could be even more grateful.

One way we could be more grateful is by being appreciative when we don't have everything we want. We might be believing God for a bigger home or nicer car, but we could take our gratefulness to the next level by expressing our appreciation for what we have right now. 1 Thessalonians 5:18 says, "Give thanks in all circumstances, for this is God's will for you in Christ Jesus."

Summary: Kids need to see our gratefulness to God. They need to see our deep appreciation of God's blessings and His kindness. They need to see our appreciation for all that we have now, not just when we get what we want. It is important to show them how to be grateful and appreciative.

Encouragement: God has given parents the upmost responsibility in being good examples of how to live. Believe it or not; children mimic the behavior of their parents. The good news is any behavior we don't like, with effort and determination, can be changed or improved. Most of us could afford to spend more time being thankful and demonstrating our gratefulness. When we show our gratefulness, it takes the focus of ourselves and glorifies God our Father. It causes us to magnify the Father, from whom all blessings come from.

Prayer: Dear Father,

Thank You for all that You have done for us. Father when we take a minute and look around, we realize that we would have nothing if it were not for You. It is not in our strength but in Yours that we have all that we have. Thank You that You push us and allow us to dream for more. For it is Your will to bless Your children, but it is not Your will that we forget to give thanks to You. It is not Your will that we become so focused on improving our lives that we become ungrateful for what You are doing right now in our present circumstances. Your Word says for us to give thanks in all circumstances. Forgive us Lord, for not giving You more thanks for the very breath that we breathe, for legs to walk, and eyes to see; we are thankful for our homes, and our jobs, and the food that we eat. Thank You Lord for our children, families, and friends. Lord thank You, that You do want us to strive for more, but thank You most importantly for what You have done and are doing in our lives right now. We thank You in advance for the good things You have in store for us as we walk with You. In Jesus' Name we pray. Amen!

Parents That Pray Praise God

Lesson Topic: Praising God

Vocabulary: praise, homage, vital

Scripture(s):   James 5:13; Psalm 106:1; Psalm 100:3-4

Lesson: James 5:13 says "Is anyone among you in
                  trouble? Let them pray. Is anyone happy?
                  Let them sing songs of praise." Many of us
                  know to pray when we are in trouble. But
                  how many of us when we are happy give
                  praise to God? Praise is defined as the act
                  of expressing approval or admiration and
                  the offering of grateful homage in words
                  or song. Grateful homage is more than
                  saying "thank You." Grateful homage
                  is deeply appreciative acknowledgment
                  (something done or given) or consideration
                  of the worth of another. Do we give deep
                  appreciation or acknowledgement for
                  what God has done in our lives?

Psalm 106:1 tells us to "Praise the Lord. Give thanks to the Lord, for He is good; His love endures forever." Why does the bible instruct us to praise God? I read in an article online that praise is a vital part of a life surrendered to God, and it gives credit where credit is due. The dictionary defines vital as necessary to life. It is necessary to our lives that we praise God. It is necessary to our lives that we give credit where credit is due.

Summary: Praise takes thankfulness to a different level. It is an outward expression of our gratitude to God. It takes our "thank You Lord" to "THANK YOU, THANK YOU, THANK YOU LORD!!" Praise is vital to our lives because it not only gives God our appreciation for His goodness, but it also does something in our spirit. It is not only uplifting to our spirits, but it also takes our minds off ourselves and puts our minds on God. Praising God and being grateful will oftentimes make you feel better.

Encouragement: We all want grateful children. We want children who realize that they are fortunate to have us and the things we provide for them. Well, so does God our Father. He desires that we give thanks. He instructs us to be thankful and say so. That means to open up our mouths and express our gratitude. It is not enough that our children are secretly grateful. How lovely it is to hear the words, "thank you. I really appreciate what you do for me." How wonderful that makes us feel. Usually, it causes us to bless our children even more. It is very important that we as parents and guardians express our gratitude and appreciation to our Father in Heaven.

Prayer: Father, we come to You lifting our hearts and our hands to You because You are worthy of our praise. You alone are the orchestrator of these most complicated bodies. You are in control of our heartbeat, the receiving and releasing of oxygen in our lungs, the blinks in our eye lids, and the electricity flowing in our brains.

You are responsible for holding up the planets. You cause the ocean to stop at the seashore. You keep us safe from dangers seen and unseen. There is none like You, Oh Lord. You heal our bodies and our broken hearts, You lift our spirits, You deliver us from evil habits, You give us favor. You are our miracle worker! You are King of Kings and Lord of Lords. You sent Jesus to die in our place, so that we could be Your children and have everlasting access to You! You are GOD Almighty! You are worthy of our praise! Help us Lord, to meditate more on all that You are and what You have done throughout time; so that we may grow in praising You! Thank You for Who You are! In Jesus' Name we pray. Amen!

Parents That Pray Do Things For Others

Lesson Topic: Doing Things For Others

Vocabulary: sacrifices

Scripture(s):   Hebrews 13:16

Lesson: God expects us to not only have faith, believe, read His Word and pray, but He expects us to help others. Hebrews 13:16 says, "And do not forget to do good and to share with others, for with such sacrifices God is pleased."

We as believers must do good. We must be aware of the hurting and those who have less than we have and get busy sharing with others. We cannot be only concerned about us and ours. Many of us have so much that we are busting at the seams. Our closets are overrun with clothes, our houses are filled with too much stuff, and in my household too many times we have so much food in the refrigerator that food goes bad because we can't see it all or have forgotten about it.

We have to start praying about how or what can we do for others. My mother started taking our excess food to a lady at church who was in need.

Summary: That food my mom took to her church member was a sacrifice. A sacrifice is the surrender of something prized or desirable for the sake of something considered as having a higher or more pressing claim.

It was a sacrifice because it was desirable food. We had more than enough, but we were still concerned about the leftovers. It also was a sacrifice because it cost her gas and her time. Many times we only want to give away things that we don't want. That's not a sacrifice. I believe God was pleased with her sacrifice because Mom considered this woman's need to be more pressing than our selfish desires to keep more than we needed and she gave up her time to take it to her.

Young people need to witness and be exposed to the importance of doing for others. They need to see us do it. They need to be included when we do it. Our giving does not always have to be things or money; sometimes the bigger sacrifices are our time.

Doing things for others produces compassion. Much needed in our schools and communities today is more compassion for others. Not only will it open our children's minds, but it opens our minds and hearts that there are many hurting and less fortunate people all around us. Being aware of that not only makes us more compassionate, but it causes us to be more grateful.

Encouragement: It is good for all of us to consider the needs of the hurting and the less fortunate. Jesus was very concerned, and we should be also.

Prayer: Lord, thank You for all that we have. Thank You Lord that many times we have more than we need. Help us Lord to really hear Your instructions and do for others in need. Increase our desire to help those not as fortunate as ourselves. Open our eyes not only to those in need but also practical ways to help. Help us to understand that it is not our job to save the world, it is only our job to use the resources (money, time, gifts/talents, health, ideas) You have given us to help someone else. For it is our desire to please You. In Jesus' Name we pray. Amen!

Parents That Pray Try To Represent God The Best They Can

Lesson Topic: Representing God The Best You Can

Vocabulary: represent; ambassadors

Scripture(s):   2 Timothy 2:15; 2 Corinthians 5:20

Lesson: Parents that are praying try their best to represent God the best way they can each day. When they fall short, they admit it, ask for forgiveness, and try again. That is a part of our walk as Christians. No one gets it all right. But as parents and those who influence children, it is important to live our lives in a way that represents God each day. One definition of represent is to portray or to present. Sometimes parents like to say, do as I say and not as I do. It is foolish to think that children are not aware of hypocritical behavior. Young people are smarter than most people think, and they are watching our every move.

A critical point in teaching them is to admit when we have messed up (and we do). This takes humility. We must teach them God's way and be honest when we fall short. In teaching them God's way, we also show them how wonderful and important forgiveness is. That even though we are Christians, we are not going to be perfect, even though we try to do our best. When we make mistakes, it is important to go to God and whoever might have been involved, admit our mistake, ask for forgiveness, and get busy trying to do our best again.

Summary: There are valuable teaching moments in our mistakes as adults. Young people need to know that we strive to do what is right and make good decisions, but sometimes we fall short. They not only need to know what they should be doing but how to handle life when they have messed up. They need to see what it looks like to admit/confess a mistake, take ownership, ask for forgiveness, and strive to do better. Not to make excuses and to avoid taking responsibility. They also need to know that when you mess up that doesn't mean that you don't strive do better.

Encouragement: How encouraging it is to know that God knows us better than we know ourselves. That He knows every mistake we've made or will make and that He chose to love us anyway. How freeing it is to know that we are forgiven for all that is past, and that we don't have to hide anything from Him. How liberating it is that we can be honest with the Father about our faults, our shortcomings, and our sins, knowing that He loves us and stands waiting to forgive us. How incredibly amazing it is that He can even use our mistakes to teach our little ones.

Prayer: Father thank You for saving us. Thank You for adopting us as Your children. Thank You for how much You love us.

You love us so much that You know every wrong thing we have ever done and will ever do and You still love us and are good to us. Thank You that when we mess up, You are waiting for us to acknowledge it, confess it, and turn away from it so that we can get on with the rest of our lives. Your Word says in 2 Corinthians 5:20 (Easy to Read Version) that, "We have been sent to speak for Christ." It is like, You God, are calling to people through us. Help us Lord to represent You well each day. Holy Spirit, continue to convict us when we miss the mark and remind us that nothing can separate us from the love of the Father, therefore we need not run from Him in fear or rebellion when we fall short. Help us to admit our mistakes and to ask for Your forgiveness right away. Then help us to feel Your love and peace so that we can recover and move on knowing that You are with us. It is a great responsibility to be Your ambassadors and we want to do a good job. Thank You for using us, Your people, to reach those who don't know You. We know that there is nothing greater in this life than knowing and being loved by You. In Jesus' Name we pray. Amen!

Parents That Pray Acknowledge Where They Are Weak

Lesson Topic: Acknowledging Where You Are Weak

Vocabulary: Weaknesses, humility

Scripture(s):   1 John 1:9; Proverbs 16:18; Proverbs 29:23

Lesson: Parents that pray are people who recognize that they are not perfect, and that they have weaknesses. There is great power in acknowledging that we make mistakes. Sometimes our mistakes are sins. Scriptures says, "If we confess our sins, He is faithful and just and will forgive our sins and purify us from all unrighteousness" (1 John 1:9). A weakness is defined as lack of strength, firmness, or vigor.

We may not get too excited about weaknesses or sins, however there is good news that if we confess our weaknesses or sins, that God is faithful and just to forgive us and help us.

The danger in this area is to not admit our weaknesses or sins. To go along acting as if we do everything right and we need no help or improvement. Proverbs 16:18 says that "Pride goeth before destruction, and a haughty spirit before a fall." We need to seek God about ourselves, our behavior, and our areas for improvement. All of us have these areas of needed improvement and all of us need to seek God about how to improve.

Proverbs 29:23 (AMP) says "Our pride and sense of self-importance will bring us down, but he who has a humble spirit will obtain honor." Humility will bring us honor. There is actually a reward in being humble. There is hope in admitting to God that we need help in a certain area.

Summary: Young people need to know that adults mess up too. They need to see that none of us are without mistakes and areas to improve. When we examine our own lives and realize how much God has forgiven us for and what we still need to improve on; it brings the gift of mercy into our lives. Mercy will cause us to be more patient with others, realizing that we are all works in progress.

Encouragement: I am encouraged in the fact that I am not perfect, cannot be perfect, and most importantly when I confess my sins and weaknesses, Scripture promises me that God is faithful and just and will forgive my sins. The freedom I receive in not having to be perfect, births compassion on others and their imperfections. It is eye-opening to realize that we all are works-in-progress.

Prayer: Dear Lord,
Thank You that You know all about us. You know our strengths and You know our weaknesses. Thank You that we don't have to pretend with You. Thank You that Your Word says in 2 Corinthians 12:9 (AMP) that "Your power is being perfected and is

completed and shows itself most effective in our weakness." Thank You God that even in our weaknesses, Your strength and Your power are so strong that it can overcome whatever weaknesses that we have. Thank You Father that we don't have to be ashamed of our weaknesses because You knew about them before we did. Our weaknesses are not a surprise to You. Thank You for the freedom in Your Word that says if we confess (admit) our sins and weaknesses that You will forgive us and help us. Forgive us for not bringing our weaknesses and sins to You, for it is not easy for us to admit our weaknesses. Thank You for Your promise to bring us through whatever is before us by Your Great Strength. We trust You and believe in You alone. In Jesus' name we pray. Amen!

Parents That Pray Forgive Others

Lesson Topic: Forgiving Others

Vocabulary: forgiveness

Scripture(s):   Matthew 6:14-15; Ephesians 4:31-32; Colossians 3:13; Romans 3:10; 1 John 1:9

Lesson: One of the biggest issues with us as believers is our unforgiveness; which is wrapped up in our bitterness, anger, and slander towards one another. We sometimes excuse it because we feel that they deserve it, and they just might. But Matthew 6:14-15 says "For if you forgive other people when they sin against you, your heavenly Father will also forgive you. But if you do not forgive others their sins, your Father will not forgive your sins." Believers, we all want our sins to be forgiven, so we must forgive.

Sometimes we say we forgive, but deep down we are still harboring some bitterness or anger towards those who have hurt us. Sometimes this is displayed directly at the one who has harmed us, other times it gets thrown on others who have nothing to do with it all. We're mad at our boss because they have been unfair in some way and then it is taken out on the kids. Ephesians 4:31-32 (NLT) instructs us to "Get rid of all bitterness, rage, anger, harsh words, and slander, as well as all types of evil behavior. Instead, be kind to each other, tenderhearted, forgiving one another, just as God through Christ has forgiven you."

None of us appreciate being yelled at or spoken to in an unkind way. Sometimes parents deal with extremely difficult and stressful situations. Sometimes that stress is expressed towards their kids. Sometimes those kids bring those hurt feelings to school and exert that same frustration on others. Other times they may withdraw all together.

Summary: Make a list of the people you are unhappy or upset with or mad at and get busy praying for help in forgiving them. Colossians 3:13 commands us "To bear with each other and forgive one another; if any of you has a grievance against someone. Forgive as the Lord forgave you."

Unforgiveness can block our blessings; it can hurt our relationships with others; it can hurt our witness; it can even make us sick. Most importantly "none of us are without sin" (Romans 3:10 ICB). So as difficult as it is many times, we have to take our hurts to Christ and be explicitly honest with Him and ask for help in forgiving.

Encouragement: We have and possess the power to forgive. Whether the offender deserves forgiveness or not, we are in control of forgiving. Someone once said, "forgiveness is really for you (the hurt). When we forgive, it begins to release us from the bondage of anger, resentment, and bitterness. I have found that forgiveness is not a one-time deal. Depending on the offense, it may have to happen several times a day for a while before freedom can occur. The good news is that it is more than worth it. It enables us to really move on and opens a door for our Father to bless us.

Prayer:

Father,

We come to You today thanking You for forgiving us for our sins and making us right with You through Jesus Christ. We acknowledge that we are not, and have never been, or will never be perfect and constantly stand in need of Your forgiveness. Thank You God that Your Word says in 1 John 1:9 (NLT) that "You are faithful and just to forgive us of our sins and cleanse us from all wickedness, if we confess our sins to You." Father, we now ask You to help us to forgive others; those who have hurt us and have not treated us right. It hurts so much Lord. Help us to forgive them that we may be able to continue to receive forgiveness from You. Help us to understand Lord, that because we need forgiveness for our sins, we must forgive others of their sins. Help us to understand how evil unforgiveness is. How unforgiveness can make us sick, unexplainably angry, and unhappy, and show us how it prevents You from doing all that You would like to do for us. Help us to see and to understand that we cannot possess an attitude that someone owes us something despite the fact of all that we owe Jesus for dying on the cross in our place for our sins. Begin to work on us in such a way that we focus more on what Jesus did for us and how much we owe Him; so much so, that we can never repay our debt. Help that understanding to breed humility and a desire to want to obey You and forgive those who have hurt us, so that You can bless us. For it is You Who restores; it is You Who can make us whole; not our offender. We trust You to deal with them and to lift the burden from us. We trust You to convict them of their wrong toward us and to help us to let it go. Remind us Lord, that we may need to confess our forgiveness of them to You a couple of times a day, for a period of time, because the hurt is so deep that it just doesn't go away immediately; but it will eventually go away as we work with and trust in You, Lord. Thank You for helping us be obedient to You and thank You for Your reward in doing so. We love You and magnify Your Holy Name. In Jesus' Name we pray. Amen!

Parents That Pray Value Family Time

Lesson Topic: Valuing Family Time

Vocabulary: time

Scripture(s):   Ephesians 5:15-16; Hebrews 13:5; Romans 12:2; 1 Peter 5:7

Lesson: Parents that pray value family time with their kids. Time spent with your kids is invaluable. Of all the things I remember about my parents and my childhood is the time we spent together. As I look back, what I think about the most and appreciate the most are the times we spent together doing things as a family. We were a working-class family. My fondest memories are drives to the mountains after church.

Ephesians 5:15-16 says, "Be very careful, then, how you live-not as unwise but as wise, making the most of every opportunity." That is a warning to us all to make good use of our time. Time can be defined as a limited period, interval, or a particular period. Young people grow up fast. The time is short (although it may not seem that way at the time) when they are young and living in your home. This time is so incredibly valuable and priceless.

Young people need more time with their families talking and sharing values. They don't need more stuff or activities but more time with those who love them the most. Sometimes parents feel they don't have time because they need to make more money. Sometimes this is true, but this should be continually prayed about. Parents have to be careful not to be overly tired and exhausted because this can lead to lack of patience with your children and lack of kindness mostly through the tone-of-voice used. Hebrews 13:5 says, "Keep your life free from the love of money and be content with what you have, for God has said, never will I leave you; never will I forsake you."

Many parents feel pressured at trying to give their kids more than they had. This can be good and other times it can rotten children. Romans 12:2 tells us, "Do not conform to the pattern of this world but be transformed by the renewing of your mind. Then you will be able to test and approve what God's will is-His good, pleasing, and perfect will."

Summary:

From a teacher's perspective, don't overload your young people with sports and other extracurricular activities and don't spoil them with more than they need. I'm not saying don't put them in any activities or reward them, I'm saying pray about these activities and gifts continually. If you are putting them in activities because of a concern you have, 1 Peter 5:7 tells us to "Cast all of our anxieties (or cares) on Him, because He cares for us." This includes the concerns of our kids.

Ask for God's guidance in determining what and how many activities they should be participating in and especially pray about how much you should shower your children with gifts beyond necessities.

Parents that pray are careful about their budget and time spent with their children. Try to do something fun and cheap at least twice a month with your children. Some suggestions are lunch at a park with a blanket, game night at home, going for walks or drives, and camping in the backyard.

Yes, activities and gifts are valuable for young people, but time spent with their parents is more valuable. More often young people are starved for time with their parents. Pray about how you can spend more time with them.

Encouragement: Parents must be aware that time with your young ones is limited. They will only be children for a limited period of their life. While you can definitely spend time with them as adults; that time in their formative years only comes once in a lifetime. While some of us have conditioned our kids to value things; deep down their true desire and utmost need is quality time with their parents. It is encouraging, especially for those who don't have a lot of disposable income, that you can spend quality time without spending a lot of money. Truthfully, when they grow up and exit your households, it won't be all the things you bought them that they remember. It will be the times spent together that will be truly valued and treasured for a lifetime.

Prayer: Dear Lord, thank You for the gift of time with our families. Help us Lord, to value more time with our kids and our families. Help us to realize how valuable this time is in our lives with our young ones. Help us to know and understand Your will when it comes to the balance of family time and extracurricular activities. Give us creativity of how we can spend more time with our children. Help us to understand more and more how much our children need our time, not just our money. Give us guidance on how to properly reward our children and give us insight when we have gotten out of balance with giving our children a little too much. Help us to be willing to make a change when You show us these things. Give us holy energy to spend the extra time with our kids that they so desperately need and desire. Help us to use our energy and time to further instill the values that You would have us to instill in each one of them so that they will be more equipped to lead lives that will be pleasing to You, Father. We depend on You for guidance, and we thank You in advance. In Jesus' Name we pray. Amen!

Parents That Pray - Pray On All Occasions

Lesson Topic: Praying On All Occasions

Vocabulary: occasions, alert, always

Scripture(s):   Ephesians 6:18

Lesson: More than ever we need parents that are praying many kinds of prayer over many things. Ephesians 6:18 says "To pray in the Spirit on all occasions with all kinds of prayers and requests. With this in mind, be alert, and always keep on praying for all of the Lord's people."

Scripture mentions to pray on all occasions. An occasion can be described as a particular time. So, all occasions would translate to all times. Our society is desperate for prayer at all times, not just in times of crisis. It goes on to state to pray with all kinds of prayers and requests. Schools are in need of prayers over things like protection over the school, budgets for schools, who to elect for the school board, and how to be involved in the school.

Also needed are prayers for the teachers, administrators, custodians, and anyone else who may come in contact with students on a daily basis. Schools need parents who are also praying for other people's kids and their parents. The end of Ephesians 6:18 instructs us "To always keep on praying for all of the Lord's people."

Summary: It's great and important to pray for and over your own child, but not all children have parents that are praying or even believing in Jesus. Not all teachers and principals believe in God. Even if they do, they need the prayers of believers. Working with young people is a demanding job. These workers are in need of strength, peace, and joy in order to teach and treat your young people right. You would not believe the pressure and stress many of these people are under and how that can affect the treatment of your children.

Parents must be alert or aware of all the different types of people that come in contact with their children. These people can have an impact, whether positive or negative, on your child at any given moment. It is vitally important to pray for them.

There are so many pieces that go into a child's education. That's why it is important that parents are always praying about everything from their child and classmates, to the teacher and principals, to the school board, and how they can be involved in the school. Everyone cannot do everything, nor is that necessary. But everyone can do something. When we seek God for guidance on what we can do, He will give us an answer.

Encouragement: Prayer is so powerful! It is one of the greatest things we can do as believers in the Lord Jesus Christ. Scripture instructs us to pray so that God can move. He needs us to do our part so that He can do His. It is a great responsibility and it is a privilege. It is an invincible wall of protections and opens doors of great blessings. It affects us and our loved ones and people around us. It changes circumstances. It moves mountains. It is conversation and communication with the Most High God. It is vital to our lives, our schools, our communities, and our world. Through prayer, lives are changed!

Prayer:

Father,

We come to You in thanksgiving, giving You thanks for all that You have done. Thank You for all that You have provided. We acknowledge Lord, that all that we have is because of You. Thank You for being so good to us. Thank You for watching over us, our families, and our loved ones. Father, we lift up to You those who will come in contact with our children. We ask that You would bless them. We ask that You would save those who don't know You. We ask that You would help them to walk in ways that are pleasing to You. Wherever they are hurting, we ask that You would heal and mend. We ask that You would bless the children in our children's classrooms. Help them to treat each other with compassion. We ask that You bless the teachers. Help them to properly juggle all the duties they have with joy and peace. Give them fresh ideas to reach our kids. We ask that You bless the administration (the principal and the assistant principals). Help them to make godly decisions. Help them to treat our children with love and respect and when they don't; convict them, Lord God. Keep them strong as they deal with a great deal of negativity throughout the school year. Help the School Board to make sound business decisions. Help them to keep our children at the forefront of their decisions and no other agendas. Bless the custodians and the cafeteria workers Lord. Help other parents that don't know You Lord, to see You. Help them with whatever they are dealing with and help them to turn to You. We ask You for Your protection of the entire school building and we plead the blood of Jesus over it. Give our children favor with everyone they come in contact with today. Thank You Lord. In Jesus' Name we pray! Amen!